Healthy Vegan Moro

While every precaution has been taken in the preparation of this book, the publisher assumes no responsibility for errors or omissions, or for damages resulting from the use of the information contained herein.

HEALTHY VEGAN MOROCCAN RECIPES

First edition. October 23, 2018.

Copyright © 2018 Bryan Rylee.

ISBN: 978-1386234999

Written by Bryan Rylee.

Introduction

The Moroccan Vegan Cuisine – Most Common Ingredients

Appetizers

Moroccan Chickpea Patties
Moroccan Carrot Dip

Moroccan Roasted Vegetables
   Moroccan Pumpkin Hummus
   Grilled Eggplants in honey and Harissa
   Moroccan Mashed Potatoes
   Salads

Moroccan Carrot-Chickpea Salad
Moroccan Lentil Salad

Moroccan-Spiced Carrot-Date Salad
   Moroccan Couscous Salad
   Moroccan Carrot Quinoa Salad with Tahini Dressing
Zaalouk

Soups and Stews

Moroccan Carrot Red Lentil Soup
Roasted Tomato Soup with Olive Toasts
Chickpea and Winter Vegetable Stew
Moroccan Red Gazpacho
Moroccan Vegetable Soup
Moroccan Harira (Bean Soup)
Moroccan Spicy Sweet Potato, Carrot, and Red Lentil Soup
Sweet and Nutty Moroccan Couscous
Quinoa stuffed baby eggplants
Sweet Potato, Chickpea and Zucchini Tagine
Vegan Moroccan Stuffed Squash
Vegan Moroccan Tagine
Couscous Shepherd's Pie
Sweet Moroccan Glazed Tofu
Vegan Berber Pizza

Desserts

Oranges with Caramel and Cardamom Syrup
Moroccan Peaches
Moroccan Apple Dessert
Moroccan Charoset Balls
Moroccan Cinnamon Cookies - Montecaos
Sfenj-Moroccan Doughnuts
Moroccan Sesame Seed cookies
Moroccan Date Bonbons
Honey Almond Stuffed Dates

Conclusion

Introduction

Dear Reader,

Thank you for choosing this recipe book, "Healthy Vegan Moroccan Recipes".

We hope it will be able to guide you through the process of enjoying healthy traditional meals, making your time in the kitchen pleasant. Recipes included in this cookbook provide you an easy way to get acquainted with Moroccan cooking culture and cook healthy and at the same time delicious vegan food, including soups, stews made of vegetables, legumes, greens, salads, as well as desserts.

Many may argue that there is no Moroccan vegan cuisine but I assure you that there is a rich variety of vegetarian meals from several cuisines you can see in that region. These tendencies influenced the way and content of what Moroccans eat. You can even see the history of the country through its food. Being a country located on the shore of the Northern Africa, it incorporates Mediterranean and Northern African traditional cuisines. But the influence on the Moroccan cuisine was not limited with the above mentioned cuisines. In Morocco you can see and feel the presence of not only Persian flavor of such stuff like saffron, nuts, pickled lemon and pomegranates but also Spanish culinary like olive, olive oil, pepper and salt which were introduced in Morocco in the Middle ages. So taking into account the richness and available diversity in Moroccan meals, we can claim certainly that the Moroccan cuisine and particularly vegetarian is one of the most balanced cuisines in the world with strong focus on flavors and aromas, wide range of spices and fresh ingredients making the Moroccan food very delicious and tasty indeed.

It's worth mentioning the hospitality of Moroccan people. In Morocco, guests are offered tea and food within seconds upon entering home. Moroccan mint tea, or as Moroccans jokingly call it, the "Moroccan whiskey", is widely consumed all across Morocco. Moroccan People drink tea all day between meals.

The main course which you will often meet in the Moroccan cuisine is couscous prepared of fine semolina grains. In Morocco, couscous is always steamed, until it is pale and fluffy. It is generally served with stewed or sautéed spicy vegetables (carrots, potatoes, turnips, *etc.*) or with some meat chicken, beef or lamb. In Morocco, couscous can be served just by itself as a main dish or as a sweet delicacy, sprinkled with raisin, toasted ground almonds, sugar and cinnamon.

The other famous dish is tagine that is traditionally cooked in clay pots known by the same name. The tagine is a rich tasty stew made of vegetables, legumes, fruit and lots of spices. In vegan versions only various vegetables, legumes fruit and nuts are added to the stew. Every part of the country has its own variety of tagine and various ways of preparing it. As it takes long to cook this meal, housewives start preparing the lunch tagine as soon as breakfast is over.

Bread (*Khobz*) is also an essential part of the Moroccan cuisine. Moroccan bread is a round and flat loaf with lots of pleasant golden crust. In some families it is baked in wood burning ovens which provide it with a unique taste. People sometimes add anise and cumin to the bread for extra flavor.

Vegetables are also an important part of Moroccan food. Carrot, potato, zucchini, onion, and pumpkin are the most common vegetables in Moroccan cooking. They are used raw, pickled or cooked in salads, soups, tagines and other dishes. Specifically, eggplant can be found in many fried dishes and many cooked vegetable salads.

As for fruits, Moroccan people eat fruit for dessert. They eat either fresh or dried fruits, such as apricot, grape, apple, plum, orange, fig, date, and peach. Fruits are often used to prepare healthy vegan desserts flavored with sweet spicy syrups.

One cannot imagine Moroccan cuisine without herbs and spices. They are used in various types, fresh or dried, whole or ground. Cilantro and parsley are the most widely used herbs in cooking and they are added to almost all dishes providing them with fresh and pleasant taste and look. The most popular among the spices are saffron, cumin, paprika, turmeric, and cinnamon, onion. Moroccan cuisine is well known for its spice mixtures. The most common among them are Harissa and Ras el Hanout. Harissa is a hot chilli paste made of various peppers, herbs and spices, such as coriander seeds, garlic paste and some olive oil or vegetable oil for preservation. Ras el Hanout is a spice blend that can be made of about 30 ground spices, but the key spices included are cinnamon, cardamom, nutmeg, anise, ginger, turmeric, various peppers, and mace.

The Moroccan Vegan Cuisine – Most Common Ingredients

Chickpeas or garbanzo beans are an important part of Moroccan cuisine. Chickpeas are rich in fiber and proteins. Beans are also perfect food for people trying to lose weight, as eating small portions keeps you full for a long time. Along with other legumes, such as lentils, split peas, beans, chickpeas are used in salads, soups, stews and tagines.

Green herbs -there are a lot of herbs used in Moroccan cuisine that provide distinct and unique flavors to any dish. But Cilantro and parsley are the most widely used herbs in Moroccan cooking and essential ingredients in fresh salads, soups, stews, etc. The other most essential herb is used to prepare the favorite Moroccan mint tea. Apart from their distinctive and fresh taste, green herbs are also a good source of vitamins and antioxidants.

Oils – olive oil is arguably the best oil to make the healthiest Moroccan dishes. They use it in seasoning salads, cooking soups, and in baking. It can also be served in a small dish or a bottle as a condiment with bread, or as a garnish for cooked salads. As the olive oil is sometimes considered very expensive for the average Moroccan, many households use vegetable oil in their cooking.

Dried Fruits and Nuts - you can find dates in many Moroccan recipes. Morocco's most commonly consumed dates are Medjoul dates; It is a sweet date with a velvety texture. They are commonly used in tagines and in making various sweet delicacies. Apart from dates, other dried fruits, such as dried apricots and raisins are used in Moroccan cooking. Walnuts and Almonds are the most commonly used nuts in the Moroccan cuisine. They are used both, as a key ingredient or as a garnish. Almonds alongside dried apricots are mostly used in making tagines as well as in preparing Moroccan amazing desserts and sweets. Nuts are a great source of fibers and healthy fats and have a rich flavor providing nice crunch to any dish.

Lemons - Lemon is another prevailing ingredient in many recipes. Both its juice and rind are edible in Moroccan culinary. Lemon juice is commonly used in preparing dressings for fresh salads. They provide a pungent citrus aroma to the sweets and desserts of Moroccan cuisine.

Saffron - is known to be the most expensive spice in the world. It is used in culinary not only for its unique taste, but also for its coloring properties. Saffron provides a nice orange color to any food that includes saffron in the ingredient list. In the Moroccan cuisine you will find saffron almost in every dish, in stews, soups, salads, and sometimes even in desserts. Store saffron in an airtight container in a dark and cool place to longer preserve its bright color and aromatic features.

Turmeric- is a bright yellow powder made from turmeric rhizomes. Turmeric has a warm and bitter taste and is used extensively as a food flavoring and dye. In Morocco, it is mainly used to make curry powders and other seasoning blends. Turmeric has a high nutritional profile. It has a good source of vitamins and minerals that are known to have antioxidant properties.

Cumin It is widely used in Moroccan cooking to season salads, beans, soups, some tagines and stews, grilled and roasted meats and more. In Morocco, *Cumin* is considered to be so essential that it is served with meal along with salt and pepper. As long as it has a strong and distinctive flavor, use it in moderate amounts when seasoning the dish. Cumin is a good source of vitamins and minerals that are known to have antioxidant properties.

Appetizers

Moroccan Chickpea Patties

These Moroccan spicy chickpea patties will melt in your mouth. Make sure you have all the ingredients at hand and get ready for this special treat.

Prep time 6 minutes
Cook time: 15 minutes
Serves 8
Ingredients:
1 small onion, diced
2-3 cloves garlic, peeled
1 tablespoon olive or vegetable oil plus a bit for frying
1 can chickpeas rinsed and drained (or 1-1.5 cups cooked)
1 lemon, juiced
1/4 cup chickpea or oat flour + 2 tablespoons for coating

2 tablespoons parsley
1 teaspoon cumin
1/4 teaspoon cinnamon
1 teaspoon salt
1/2 teaspoon ground coriander
1/4 teaspoon cayenne
1/4 teaspoon black pepper
1/4 teaspoon ground ginger

Directions:

1. Heat the olive oil in a medium frying pan over medium-high heat.
2. Add the garlic and onion and sauté until the onions are golden and translucent, about 4 minutes.
3. Add the chickpeas to a microwave safe bowl and heat 2 minutes on High, until heated through.
4. Place the warm chickpeas, cooked onions, chickpea flour, garlic, parsley lemon juice, cinnamon, cumin, cayenne, coriander, ginger and black pepper in a blender.
5. Pulse until the mixture resembles smooth thick paste.
6. Using your hands shape patties and coat them with flour.
7. Add a few tablespoons of oil to a large nonstick skillet and set over a medium heat.
8. Once it starts sizzling, place the patties in the hot oil and fry for about 3 minutes per side until patties acquire golden crust.
9. Serve the burgers with fresh veggie salad or on a bun.

Moroccan Carrot Dip

Carrots are very popular in Moroccan cuisine, and it is valued for the health benefits, that it provides. In this dish, a new preparation method is suggested. Make sure not to brown carrots when cooking to get a nice orange color.

Prep time: 40 minutes
Cook time: 25 minutes
Serves: 2-4 servings
Ingredients:
3 tablespoons extra-virgin olive oil
2 lbs carrots (about 12), peeled and sliced
2 garlic cloves, minced
3/4 teaspoon ground coriander
3/4 teaspoon ground cumin
3/4 teaspoon ground ginger
1/8 teaspoon chili powder
1/8 teaspoon ground cinnamon
1/3 cup water
1 tablespoon white wine vinegar
1 tablespoon minced fresh cilantro
Salt
Pepper
Directions:

1. Add 1 tablespoon of the olive oil to a large griddle and set over medium-high heat.
2. Once sizzling, add the carrots and 1/2 teaspoon salt and cook until crisp-tender, 4-6 minutes.
3. Stir in the cumin, garlic, cinnamon coriander, chili powder and ginger and sauté until fragrant, about half a minute. Add the water and bring to a boil.

4. Then slow down the heat to low, and let simmer, covered, stirring often, until the carrots are tender, 18- 20 minutes.
5. Remove the griddle from the heat and using a potato masher, mash the carrots.
6. Add the vinegar and remaining 2 tablespoons oil. Transfer to a bowl and chill in the refrigerator for 25 minutes, covered.
7. Season them with salt and pepper to taste, garnish with chopped cilantro and enjoy.
8. The dip can be refrigerated in an airtight container for up to 2 days. Season with additional vinegar, salt and pepper to taste and sprinkle with the cilantro before serving.

Moroccan Roasted Vegetables

These roasted vegetables flavored with Moroccan spices are an easy side for vegan dinner party. Try to cut the red pepper into thin strips as they provide a pleasant lookto this dish.

Prep Time: 20 minutes
Cook Time: 40 minutes
Serves 6
1 medium onion cut in slices
1 medium zucchini cut in half moons
1 small eggplant, peeled, cut into half moons
1 large sweet potato, peeled, cut into half moons
1 large red pepper, sliced in 1/4-inch strips
2 medium tomatoes, fresh, chopped
15 oz. (420 g) chickpeas, drained and rinsed
3 garlic cloves, minced
2 tablespoons olive oil

1 tablespoon lemon juice
1 tablespoon cumin
1 1/2 teaspoons turmeric
1 1/2 teaspoons cinnamon
1 1/2 teaspoons paprika
1/4 teaspoon cayenne

Directions:

1. Place the zucchini, eggplant, onion, potato, red pepper, tomatoes, chickpeas and garlic in a large salad bowl.
2. In a small bowl, mix together the lemon juice, cumin, turmeric, cinnamon, paprika, cayenne and olive oil.
3. Pour the mixture over the vegetables and toss to combine.
4. Place the vegetables in a rimmed baking dish and bake in the oven for about 35-40 minutes, stirring 2-3 times.

Moroccan Pumpkin Hummus

Prep time: 10 minutes
Cook time: 5 minutes
Serves 4-6

Hummus is arguably the healthiest dip that you can feel free to indulge in. It is delicious with grilled pita bread, carrots or even simply whole wheat crackers. And tahini is typically what makes hummus taste like hummus.

Ingredients:
1 tablespoon olive oil
2 garlic cloves, chopped
1 teaspoon ground ginger
1 teaspoon ground coriander
1/4 teaspoon cinnamon
1/4 teaspoon ground allspice
1/4 teaspoon turmeric
1/8 teaspoon cayenne
1/4 teaspoon sugar
2 tablespoons tahini
1 cup home-cooked or canned chickpeas
1 cup canned solid-pack pumpkin (or fresh cooked winter squash or pumpkin!)
2 tablespoons fresh lemon juice
1/2 teaspoon salt
1/4 teaspoon black pepper
1 tablespoon pistachios, chopped for garnish

Directions:

1. Add 1 tablespoon olive to a frying pan and set over medium heat.
2. Add the ginger, garlic, cinnamon, coriander, turmeric, allspice,

cayenne, and sugar and sauté for 1-2 minutes.
3. Add the chickpeas and tahini, give a stir and then remove the pan from the heat.
4. Add the lemon juice, pumpkin, season with salt and pepper. Let cool.
5. Add the mixture to a food processor and pulse until smooth.
6. Place the hummus into a serving bowl, sprinkle with the chopped pistachios and serve.
7. Great to chill for a couple of hours before serving.

Grilled Eggplants in honey and Harissa

The amazing flavors of eggplant and honey are paired with harissa in this satisfying tasty dish. Enjoy with freshly cooked rice.

Prep time: 5 minutes
Cook time: 18 minutes
Serves 4
Ingredients:
2 eggplants, peeled and thickly sliced
Olive oil for frying
2-3 garlic cloves, crushed
2- inch piece of fresh root ginger, peeled and grated
1 teaspoon ground cumin
1 teaspoon harissa
3 tablespoons honey
Juice of 1 lemon
Sea salt

Directions:

1. Preheat the grill to medium. Coat the eggplant slices with olive oil and grill on both sides, until lightly golden.
2. Heat little olive oil in a large skillet over medium heat. Add the garlic and sauté for 30 seconds.
3. Add the cumin, ginger, honey, lemon juice and harissa and stir fry for a few seconds.
4. Add enough water so that it covers the base of the skillet, and arrange the eggplant slices in the skillet. Let cook until all liquid is absorbed, about 10 minutes. Add little extra water if needed. Season with salt and let cool.
5. Serve the dish with fresh bread. .

Moroccan Mashed Potatoes

If you are fond of potato, then this Moroccan dish would serve your appetite ideally. The addition of spices gave it an unforgettable taste.

Prep time: 20 minutes
Cook time: 15 minutes
Serves 32
Ingredients:
10 largebaking potatoes, peeled and cubed

3 tablespoonsolive oil, or as needed
1onion, diced
1 tablespoonground turmeric
1 tablespoonsalt, or to taste
2 teaspoonsground black pepper
1/2 teaspoonground cumin

Directions:

1. Put the potatoes into a large saucepan; pour in enough water to cover and bring to a boil over medium-high heat.
2. Cook for about 23-25 minute, until potatoes are soft.
3. Add 1 tablespoon olive oil to a frying pan and set over medium-high heat.
4. Add the onion and sauté until golden and translucent, about 5minutes.
5. Pour off the potato cooking liquid and mash the potatoes, add the cooked onion, cumin, turmeric, season with salt and pepper and continue mashing.
6. Add the remaining 2 tablespoons of olive oil and stir well to make creamy puree.

Salads

Moroccan Carrot-Chickpea Salad

This is a fantastic salad and can be served with any main course. It goes well with greens and rice. It is very tasty and aromatic, let alone the benefits of carrots, raisins and cashews.

Prep time: 20 minutes
Cook time:0 minutes
Serves 8
Ingredients:
Zest and juice of 1 lemon
1 teaspoon ground coriander
1/8 teaspoon cayenne pepper
1 ¼ teaspoon salt
1/3 cup Extra Virgin Olive oil
1 ½ lbs (700 g) carrots, coarsely grated
2 cans (15 oz.) chickpeas, rinsed
1/2 cup golden raisins
1/2 cup roasted, unsalted cashews, coarsely chopped
1/3 cup coarsely chopped cilantro, plus leaves for garnish
1/3 cup fresh mint, chopped
Directions;

1. In a large salad bowl, whisk together the olive oil, lemon zest and juice, cayenne, coriander and 1 1/4 teaspoon of salt.
2. Add the chickpeas, carrots, cashews, raisins, mint and chopped cilantro and mix to combine. Let stand for at least 10 minutes. Garnish the salad with cilantro leaves and serve.

Moroccan Lentil Salad

The combination of garbanzo beans, tomatoes and colorful peppers flavored with lemon juice makes this salad delicious and a first choice of people looking for a healthy food.

Prep time: 40 minutes
Cook time: 40minutes
Serves 5
Ingredients:
1/2 cup dry lentils
1 1/2 cups water
1/2 (15 ounce) can garbanzo beans, drained
2 tomatoes, chopped
4 green onions, chopped
2 hot green chili peppers, minced
1 green bell pepper, chopped
1/2 yellow bell pepper, chopped

1 red bell pepper, chopped
1 lime, juiced
2 tablespoons olive oil
1/4 cup fresh cilantro, chopped
Salt to taste

Directions:

1. Add lentils to a medium saucepan, pour in the water and set over medium-high heat.
2. Once boiling, slow down the heat and let simmer, until soft, about 30 minutes.
3. Place the cooked lentils, green onions, tomatoes, chickpeas, bell peppers, green chilies in a medium salad bowl, add the olive oil, lime juice and chopped cilantro.
4. Season the salad with salt to taste and mix well to combine.
5. Refrigerate for 30 minutes before serving.

Moroccan-Spiced Carrot-Date Salad

This is a wonderful salad full of refreshing flavors. Make sure you have all the ingredients on hand and start experiencing.

Prep Time: 45 minutes
Cook Time: 5 minutes
Serves: 6
Ingredients:
Salad:
1 lb (450 g) carrots, grated
1 oz. (30 g) fresh flat leaf parsley, coarsely chopped (about ½ cup chopped)
1 medium white onion, halved and thinly sliced
4 medium Medjool dates, pitted, halved, and thinly sliced cross-wise
2 medium navel oranges, peeled and sliced cross-wise
Dressing:
3 tablespoons fresh lemon juice
3 tablespoons olive oil
2 medium cloves garlic, crushed
½ teaspoon salt
½ teaspoon ground sweet paprika
¼ teaspoon ground coriander
¼ teaspoon ground black pepper
⅛ teaspoon ground cinnamon
Directions:

1. Using a mandolin, thinly slice the carrots into ribbons and transfer to a large bowl of ice water. Let them stand for 20-25 minutes, until curled
2. Remove from the water and drain. Place the carrots in a large bowl, add the oranges, dates, onion and chopped parsley.
3. In a small bowl, mix together the olive oil, lemon juice, garlic,

paprika, coriander, cinnamon,
4. Pour the dressing over the salad and mix to combine.
5. Enjoy.

Moroccan Couscous Salad

This is a very simple, but very tasty Moroccan dish. The mandarin oranges, chickpeas and bell peppers provide it a wonderful flavor and look.

Prep Time: 15 minutes
Cook Time: 5 minutes
Servings: 6-8

Ingredients:
1/4cup peanut oil or 1/4cupolive oil
1/4teaspoonturmeric
1/4teaspooncinnamon
1/4teaspoonground ginger
1/4teaspooncumin
1/4teaspooncayenne
1 1/2-2 cupscouscous
2 1/2cupswater or 2 1/2cupsvegetable stock

1/4 cup orange juice
1-2 tablespoon brown sugar
1 (15 oz. /420 g) can chickpeas
1 (8 oz./230 g) can mandarin oranges
1 red onion, chopped
1 green bell peppers or 1 red bell pepper, chopped
1/4 cup golden raisin
2-3 tablespoons fresh cilantro
2 tablespoons peanuts (optional) or 2 tablespoons almonds (optional)
Salt

Directions:

1. Add 1 tablespoon of oil to a medium pot and set over medium-high heat. Add the turmeric, cumin, cayenne, ginger, cinnamon and uncooked couscous and stir fry until fragrant, about 1-2 minutes.
2. Pour in the vegetable stock and bring to a boil.
3. Slow down the heat, put the lid on and let simmer until all liquid is absorbed, about 5 minutes. Turn off the heat and let stand about 5 minutes.
4. Using a fork, gently fluff the couscous and transfer it to a medium salad bowl. Add the onion, bell peppers, chickpeas, mandarin oranges and raisins.
5. Make the dressing by combining orange juice, sugar and 3 tablespoons oil in a small bowl. Season the dressing with salt and pour over the salad. Mix well to combine,
6. Sprinkle the salad with nuts and cilantro. Chill for about 30 minutes and enjoy.

Moroccan Carrot Quinoa Salad with Tahini Dressing

Sweet from maple syrup, sour from lemon and flavored with lots of spices, this humble salad manages to get all taste buds firing at once.

Prep Time: 45 minutes
Cook Time: 5 minutes
Serves: 4
Ingredients:
4 carrots
5 oz. (150 g) cooked chickpeas
1/4 cup uncooked quinoa
5 oz. (150 g) potatoes (about 3-4 small)
6 1/3 oz. (180 g) cauliflower
1 ½ oz.(40 g) dried figs
1 teaspoon pine nuts
1 teaspoon olive oil
1 teaspoon cumin
1/8 teaspoon sweet smoked paprika
a pinch of spicy paprika
For the dressing
1 teaspoon extra virgin olive oil
1 teaspoon tahini
1 teaspoon maple syrup (or honey)
1 teaspoon lemon juice
Handful of parsley
Directions:

1. Cook the potatoes in a medium pot until soft.
2. Cook the quinoa following the package instructions.
3. Add 1 teaspoon of olive oil to a large frying pan and heat over medium heat. Add the chopped potatoes, chickpeas,

cauliflower, and cooked quinoas, season with paprika, cumin and salt and pepper to taste.
4. Using a mandolin or a vegetable peeler, thinly slice the carrots into ribbons.
5. Cut figs into smaller pieces.
6. Place all salad ingredients in a bowl and pour the dressing over the salad.

Zaalouk

Very tasty and traditional Moroccan salad. Add some freshly squeezed lemon juice to the salad to make the taste complete.

Prep time: 10 minutes
Cook time: 50 minutes
Serves 4
Ingredients:
2 large eggplants
3 large tomatoes
2-3 garlic cloves peeled and chopped
½ cup good olive oil
1 tablespoon of fresh coriander chopped
1/2 tsp sweet paprika
Juice of 1 lemon (or to taste)
Ground cumin to serve
Salt

Directions:

1. Preheat the oven to 400 F (200 C).
2. Place the eggplants on a baking sheet and bake in the oven until tender, about 25 minutes.
3. Place the tomatoes in a roasting tin, with 1/4 cup of the olive oil and roast for 5-10 minutes.
4. Withdraw the eggplants and tomatoes from the oven and let cool. Halve the baked eggplants, scoop out the pulp with a spoon and chop.
5. Remove the skin and seeds from tomatoes, and chop the pulp. Skin the tomatoes and remove the seed and chop the flesh also to a pulp.
6. Add the remaining oil to a medium skillet and set over moderate heat. Add the garlic and sauté for a few seconds.
7. Add the eggplants, tomatoes and paprika and cook for 8-10 minutes, stirring frequently. In the end, add the coriander, salt and lemon juice, gently stir to combine.
8. Place the salad in a serving bowl, sprinkle with cumin and serve with fresh bread.
9. Great to enjoy warm or at room temperature.

Soups and stews

Moroccan Carrot Red Lentil Soup

Prep time 10 minutes

Cook time 35 minutes

Serves: 8

Easy and tasty soup full of healthy vegetables and spices. This dishis perfect especially for cold winter.

Ingredients:

2 tablespoons olive oil

1 sweet onion, chopped
3 garlic cloves, minced
7 carrots, peeled, chopped
1 teaspoon cumin
1 teaspoon turmeric
2 teaspoon coriander
½ teaspoon paprika
¼ teaspoon cinnamon
2 cups red lentils, rinsed until water runs clear
1-15 oz can diced tomatoes
6 cups vegetable broth
Salt and pepper, to taste
Fresh cilantro, fresh lemon juice and crushed red pepper, to garnish
Directions:

1. Add 2 tablespoons of olive oil to a large saucepan and place over medium heat.
2. Add the garlic and onion and sauté until tender.
3. Stir in the carrots and sauté until carrots have softened, about 10 minutes.
4. Add the cinnamon, cumin, coriander, paprika, turmeric and cook for another 2 minutes.
5. Add the diced tomatoes, lentils and vegetable broth, give a stir to combine and let simmer over low heat until lentils are soft, for about 35 minutes.
6. To make a creamy soup, blend it in portions or you may use an immersion blender.
7. Ladle the soup into serving bowls, sprinkle with fresh cilantro and red pepper.
8. Serve with fresh lemon juice.

Roasted Tomato Soup with Olive Toasts

This delicious soup is full of great flavors. It looks nice and tastes great.

Prep time 20 minutes

Cook time: 1 hr 30 minutes

Serves 8

Ingredients:

2 1/4 lbs (1100 g) plum tomatoes cut in half lengthwise

2 garlic cloves, unpeeled

2 medium sweet onions, thinly sliced

1/2 red bell pepper, seeded

Cooking spray

1 1/2 teaspoons olive oil

1/2 teaspoon ground cumin

1/2 teaspoon ground coriander

1 teaspoon harissa

1/4 teaspoon Spanish smoked paprika

2 1/2 cups vegetable broth

1/2 cup water

1/2 teaspoon fresh thyme, chopped

1 1/2 teaspoons fresh lemon juice

1/8 teaspoon salt

1/8 teaspoon freshly ground black pepper

Toasts:

1 garlic clove, halved

8 (1/4-inch-thick) slices of French bread baguette, toasted

1/4 cup pitted Kalamata olives, chopped

1 1/2 teaspoons chopped fresh parsley

1/4 teaspoon balsamic vinegar

1/8 teaspoon fresh thyme, chopped

Directions:

1. Preheat oven to 425°F (220 °C).
2. Coat a baking sheet with cooking spray. Place the halved tomatoes, cut sides up, 2 garlic onion slices, cloves, and bell pepper half on the prepared baking sheet and bake in the oven until brown, about 60-70 minutes. Remove from the oven and let cool.
3. Cut the onion, tomatoes, and bell pepper. Reserve 1/3 cup chopped onion for the toasts. Squeeze the baked garlic cloves to extract pulp and discard the skins.
4. Add the olive oil to a griddle and set over medium heat.
5. Stir in the bell pepper, remaining chopped onion, cumin and coriander; sauté for 5 minutes, stirring often.
6. Stir in the paprika and harissa, cook for another 2-3 minutes.
7. Add the garlic pulp, tomatoes, water, broth, and 1/2 teaspoon thyme; bring to a boil.
8. Slow down the heat and let simmer, covered, 12-15 minutes.
9. Add the lemon juice, season with salt and black pepper and let stand 5 minutes.
10. Blend the tomato soup in a food processor in 2 batches until smooth.
11. Make the toasts. Rub one side of each baguette slice with halved garlic clove.
12. In a small bowl, mix together the olives, vinegar, 1/8 teaspoon thyme, parsley and reserved 1/3 cup chopped onion. Place about 1 tablespoon olive mixture onto each bread slice and spread evenly.
13. Ladle the soup into serving bowls and serve with an olive toast.

Chickpea and Winter Vegetable Stew

A nice combination of vegetables and spices. And it is also rich in proteins and vitamins. This stew is very filling and perfect for lunch or dinner.

Prep time 15 minutes
Cook time 40 minutes
Serves 8

Ingredients:

2 teaspoons extra-virgin olive oil
1 cup chopped onion
1 cup (1/2-inch) slices leek
1/2 teaspoon ground coriander
1/2 teaspoon caraway seeds, crushed
1/8 teaspoon cumin, ground
1/8 teaspoon red pepper, ground
1 garlic clove, minced
3 2/3 cups vegetable stock, divided
2 cups (1-inch) butternut squash, peeled, cubed
1 cup (1/2-inch) slices carrot
3/4 cup (1-inch) Yukon gold potato, peeled, cubed
1 tablespoon harissa
1 1/2 teaspoons tomato paste
3/4 teaspoon salt
1 lb. (450 g) turnips, peeled and each cut into 8 wedges
1 (15 1/2-ounce) can chickpeas, drained
1/4 cup fresh flat-leaf parsley, chopped
1 1/2 teaspoons honey
1 1/3 cups uncooked couscous
8 lemon wedges

Directions:

1. Add the olive oil to a large pot and set over medium-high heat.
2. Add the leek and onion and cook for 5 minutes. Add the caraway seeds, coriander, cumin, red pepper and garlic and stir-fry for a minute.
3. Add the butternut squash, carrots, potato, tomato paste, harissa, turnips and salt, pour in 3 cups of vegetable stock and bring the mixture to a boil.
4. Slow down the heat and let simmer, covered, about 30 minutes.
5. Stir in the honey and chopped parsley.
6. Take 2/3 cup hot cooking liquid from the butternut squash mixture and transfer to a medium bowl. Pour in the remaining 2/3 cup stock, as well.
7. Add the couscous, give a stir and let stand for 5 minutes, covered. Fluff the couscous with a fork.
8. Serve the stew over the cooked couscous, sprinkled with fresh cilantro leaves.
9. Serve with lemon wedges.

Moroccan Red Gazpacho

So many culinary wonders and all in your hands. Sure, you don't want to miss out this hot and spicy treat.

Prep time; 2 Hours,5 Minutes
Cook time: 5 minutes
Serves 8

Ingredients

1 (6 1/2-inch) pita, torn into pieces
1/2 cup boiling water
4 tablespoons extra-virgin olive oil, divided
2 tablespoons sherry vinegar
4 large ripe plum tomatoes, coarsely chopped (about 1 pound)
1 large red bell pepper, seeded and coarsely chopped
1 large cucumber, peeled, seeded, and coarsely chopped (about 8 ounces)
1/4 small yellow onion, chopped
2 cups no-salt-added tomato puree
1 cup cold water
2 teaspoons Ras el Hanout
3/4 teaspoon salt
1/2 teaspoon ground cumin
1/4 teaspoon ground cinnamon
2 tablespoons fresh cilantro, chopped

Directions:

1. Put the pita in a large shallow bowl; add 1/2 cup boiling water and let stand for 1-2 minutes.
2. Remove the moistened pita from the bowl and transfer to a food processor.
3. Add the tomatoes, cucumber, red bell pepper, sherry vinegar, 1 tablespoon oil and onion and process until smooth.
4. Add the tomato puree, water, Ras el Hanout, salt, cinnamon and cumin.
5. Refrigerate for 2 hours, covered
6. Pour the soup into serving bowls; drizzle each with 1 teaspoon oil, garnish with 3/4 teaspoon chopped cilantro.
7. Enjoy.

Moroccan Vegetable Soup

Including a great combination of healthy vegetables, this dish is a real arsenal of vitamins and nutrients.

Prep time: 15 minutes
Cook time: 55 minutes
Serves 5
Ingredients:
2 tablespoonsolive oil
1onion, chopped
1 cupcarrots, peeled, chopped
1 cupparsnips, peeled, chopped
1 cupcanned pumpkin puree
4 cupsvegetable stock
1 teaspoonlemon juice
Black pepper, ground (to taste)
Salt to taste
1/2 teaspoondried cilantro
2 teaspoonsolive oil (optional)
1 clovegarlic, minced(optional)
3 tablespoonschopped fresh parsley (optional)
1/8 teaspoonpaprika (optional)

Directions:

1. Add 2 tablespoons olive oil to a large saucepan and set over medium-high heat.
2. Add the onions and sauté, stirring frequently, until the onion is tender and translucent, about 5 minutes.
3. Add the parsnips and carrots, put the lid on and let cook until vegetables are crisp-tender, about 5 minutes.
4. Pour in the stock and pumpkin puree and bring the soup to a simmer over low heat, about 40 minutes. When the vegetables are soft, add the lemon juice and cilantro, and season the soup with salt and pepper.
5. Remove the saucepan from the heat and let cool.
6. Blend the soup in batches in a food processor until smooth. Add more stock if the soup is too thick.
7. Make the garnish. In a small frying pan, heat the olive oil over medium-low heat. Add the garlic and parsley and sauté for 1-2 minutes. Stir in the paprika. Add about 1/2 teaspoon of the garnish into each serving of soup.

I love this soup. Great on a cold rainy day. I add cayenne pepper to bowl right before serving and it adds a nice heat

Moroccan Harira (Bean Soup)

If you are looking for soup with a real Moroccan flavor, then you must try Harira. The addition of beans, tomatoes and herbs makes it a healthy and tasty dish.

Prep time: 15 minutes
Cook time: 1 hr
Serves 10
Ingredients:
6 cups water
1 cup dry lentils
1 tablespoon olive oil, or to taste
1 onion, chopped
1 cinnamon stick
1 teaspoon minced fresh ginger root
1 teaspoon ground turmeric
1 teaspoon ground cumin

1 teaspoon ground black pepper
1 (15 ounce) can garbanzo beans, drained
1 (15 ounce) can red kidney beans, rinsed and drained
1 (14 ounce) can diced tomatoes
1 cup cooked quinoa (optional)
1 bunch flat-leaf parsley leaves and thinner stems, chopped
1 bunch cilantro leaves and thinner stems, chopped
1 lemon, or to taste, juiced

Directions:

1. Combine the water and lentils together in a large saucepan and set over medium-high heat.
2. Once it boils, slow down the heat to low, and let simmer.
3. Add the olive oil to a frying pan and set over medium heat.
4. Add the ginger, onion, cinnamon stick, cumin, black pepper and turmeric and sauté l until the onion is tender and translucent, about 5 minutes. Add this mixture to lentils mixture.
5. Add the tomatoes, quinoa, garbanzo beans and kidney beans, give a stir and continue cooking. When the mixture begins to boil, add the cilantro and parsley and let simmer over low heat until the lentils are soft, for about 45 minutes.
6. Ladle the soup into serving bowl, drizzle with lemon juice and serve.

Moroccan Spicy Sweet Potato, Carrot, and Red Lentil Soup

This spicy red lentil soup is delicious anytime. The addition of carrots and cilantro adds a nice color and fresh look to this soup.

Prep time 10 minutes
Cook time 35 minutes
Serves: 6-8

Ingredients:
2 tablespoons olive oil
1 large sweet yellow onion, chopped
1 large sweet potato, peeled and chunked
5 to 6 large carrots, peeled and chunked (about 4 cups)
1 cup red lentils
8 cups vegetable stock
1 tablespoon Harissa paste
2 teaspoons Ras el Hanout
1 teaspoon salt
1/2 teaspoon pepper
Nigella seeds (or black caraway) for garnish
Cilantro, chopped, for garnish

Directions:

1. Heat the olive oil in large griddle over moderate heat. Add the onions and sauté minutes until tender and translucent, about 7 minutes.
2. Add the carrots, potatoes, lentils, harissa paste, ras el hanout, salt and pepper, pour in the vegetable stock and bring to a boil.
3. Slow down the heat and let simmer, covered, until the lentils, potatoes and carrots are tender, 20-25 minutes. Remove from the heat and let cool.
4. Blend the soup in batches until creamy and smooth. Adjust

seasonings to taste.
5. Pour the soup into serving bowls, sprinkle with chopped cilantro and Nigella seeds.
6. Enjoy.

Main Dishes

Sweet and Nutty Moroccan Couscous

Couscous is a traditional Moroccandish that has various ways of preparing it. Sure, you will enjoy this healthy version of preparation with dried apricots, dates and almonds.

Prep time: 15 minutes
Cook time: 5 minutes
Serves 6
Ingredients:
2 cups vegetable broth
5 tablespoons olive oil
1/3 cup chopped dates
1/3 cup chopped dried apricots
1/3 cup golden raisins
2 cups dry couscous

3 teaspoons ground cinnamon
1/2 cup slivered almonds, toasted
Directions:

1. Add the vegetable broth into a large pot and bring to a boil over medium-high heat.
2. Add the olive oil, dates, apricots and raisins and cook for 2-3 minutes.
3. Remove the pot from the heat, and add the couscous.
4. Put the lid on and let sit for 5 minutes.
5. Add the toasted almonds and cinnamon, stir to combine and serve.

Quinoa stuffed baby eggplants

My family adores this dish. Prepared with eggplants, quinoa and tomatoes and flavored with tons of spices, this dish cannot leave anyone indifferent. It is always a hit at the family gatherings.

Prep time: 20 minutes
Cook time: 45 minutes
Serves: 6
Ingredients:
Olive oil
1/2 tsp cloves (whole)
2-3 bay leaves
1 medium onion, chopped
1 tsp cumin seeds
1 tsp coriander powder
1/4 tsp cloves, ground
1/2 tsp cinnamon, ground
2-3 garlic cloves, minced
8-9 baby eggplants
1 cup quinoa, uncooked
1 tsp paprika
1 can of tomatoes
½ cup water
2 tablespoons sunflower seeds (or pine nuts)
1/2 cup raisins
1 cup tomato juice
1 cup water
Sea salt, to taste
Freshly ground pepper, to taste
Chili flakes

HEALTHY VEGAN MOROCCAN RECIPES

Directions:

1. Heat the olive oil in a large skillet and place over low heat. Add the cloves and bay leaves and stir-fry for 1-2 minutes, until lightly brown.
2. Remove the spices from the skillet. Add the onion, cook for about 2 minutes.
3. Then add the coriander powder, cumin seeds and cinnamon and cook over medium heat until the onion has softened.
4. Meanwhile scoop out the baby eggplant flesh and cut into small cubes.
5. Add the cubed eggplant and garlic to the skillet and sauté, stirring frequently, about 10 minutes. Add more oil, if necessary.
6. Place the tomatoes, uncooked quinoa, paprika and ½ cup water in a medium bowl and mix to combine.
7. When the eggplant is al dente, add the quinoa mix to the skillet and cook over medium heat, covered, for 5 minutes.
8. Remove the cover and let the mixture cook until the liquid is evaporated and the quinoa is crisp-tender.
9. Remove the skillet from the heat, and add the raisins and sunflower seeds sprinkle the stuffing with chili flakes and salt and pepper.
10. Fill the eggplants with the stuffing and cover with their own stems.
11. Gently place them in a Dutch oven, tightly close to each other, so they stay upright.Add 1 cup tomato juice, 1 cup water, sprinkle some olive oil over the eggplants and cook over medium heat, about 20 minutes, until the quinoa is tender.

Sweet Potato, Chickpea and Zucchini Tagine

This is an authentic dish that tastes like it came straight from a five star Moroccan restaurant! Serve it hot over couscous and enjoy.

Prep time: 10 minutes
Cook time: 35 minutes
Serves: 4

Ingredients:
2 sweet potatoes, peeled and cubed
1 zucchini, chopped
14 oz. (400g) tin of chickpeas, drained and rinsed
2 green bell peppers
1 large onion, chopped
4 cloves of garlic, finely chopped
1 tablespoon of ginger, peeled and grated
2 teaspoons sweet paprika
2 teaspoons of smoked paprika
2 teaspoons ground coriander
2 teaspoons ground cumin
1 teaspoon chili powder
1 teaspoon cinnamon
½ teaspoon ground cardamom
½ teaspoon allspice
3 tablespoons of olive oil
1 cup of vegetable stock
¼ cup of apricots, chopped
¼ cup of fresh coriander, chopped
Flaked or slivered almonds to serve

Directions:

1. Preheat the oven to 450 °F (230 °C)
2. Place the sweet potato and 1 tablespoon of olive oil in a bowl and toss to coat.
3. Transfer to a rimmed baking pan.
4. Place the bell peppers in a roasting pan. Place both pans in the oven and bake for 25- 30 minutes, until the sweet potato is soft when pierced with a fork and the bell peppers become light brown.
5. Let cool. Remove the skin of bell peppers and chop peppers into thin strips.
6. Place a large casserole dish over medium-high heat. Add the olive oil, garlic, onion, ginger, and spices. Sauté until the onions are tender and golden-brown and the spices are fragrant.
7. Stir in the zucchini and cook until just-tender.
8. Stir in the sweet potato, apricots, the vegetable stock, chickpeas, and green peppers and bring the mixture to a boil.
9. Slow down the heat and let simmer for 8-10 minutes.
10. Pour the tagine into serving bowls, sprinkle with chopped coriander and almonds.
11. Enjoy

Vegan Moroccan Stuffed Squash

This recipe makes an authentic Moroccan dish, perfect for lunch and dinner. Carrots, chickpeas, squash and onion, as well as fresh dries apricots and nuts make this dish healthy and full of flavor.

Prep time: 15 minutes
Cook time: 70 minutes
Serves 4-6
Ingredients;
2 large squash (butternut, small pumpkin)
2 medium (150 g) tomatoes diced
1 medium carrot peeled, thinly chopped
1 cup (150 g)chickpeas, cooked/canned, drained
1/2 cup hazelnuts or walnuts, chopped

1/4 cup dried apricots, chopped
3 tablespoons olive oil
1 medium onion, chopped
2 cloves garlic finely chopped
1/2 teaspoon fresh ginger finely, chopped
1/2 teaspoon black pepper
1/2 teaspoon paprika
1/2 teaspoon ground cinnamon or 1-2 small sticks cinnamon bark
1 teaspoon turmeric
3/4 teaspoon salt
2 1/2 cups vegetable stock or water + 2 tablespoons vegetable broth powder
1 cup couscous (uncooked)
Directions:

1. Preheat oven to 400°F (200°C). Lightly coat a baking sheet with oil.
2. Halve the squash in lengthwise. Using a spoon, remove soft insides and arrange on the baking sheet, hollowed side up.
3. Roast in the oven for 20 minutes.
4. Sauté the garlic, onion, ginger, nuts, paprika and pepper in the heated oil over moderate heat about 3 minutes.
5. Stir in the tomatoes, chickpeas, carrots, apricots / raisins, turmeric and cinnamon and cook for another 3 minutes.
6. Add the vegetable broth powder, salt, vegetable stock or water and bring the mixture to a boil. Let cook for 5 minutes stirring constantly.
7. Add the couscous and bring to a simmer over low heat, stirring frequently, until the couscous is tender, 6-7 minutes.
8. Once the squash halves are done, remove from the oven and fill with vegetable couscous stuffing.
9. Bake the stuffed squash in the oven until squash is done, about

30-35 minutes.
10. Garnish the dish with chopped fresh parsley and chopped nuts, season with ground paprika and serve.

Vegan Moroccan Tagine

This dish is a vegan version of tagine, full of healthy vegetables and flavors that work together well and create a tasty and hearty meal. Serve it with bread or couscous and enjoy.

Prep time: 20 minutes
Cooking time: 30 minutes
Serves 4
Ingredients:
1 cup garbanzo beans, cooked
1 small eggplant, diced
1 red bell pepper, diced
1 medium zucchini, sliced
1 large potato, peeled and diced
1 large onion, sliced
1 cup sliced mushrooms
1 carrot, peeled and diced

3 medium tomatoes, pureed
4 cloves garlic, minced
¼ cup fresh parsley, roughly chopped
¼ cup golden raisins or sultanas
2 tablespoons olive oil
1 tablespoon ground cumin,
½ tbsp coriander, ground
3 tsp sugar
Cinnamon stick
Sea salt
Dried red chili flakes (optional)

Directions:

1. Heat the olive oil in a large saucepan over medium-high heat.
2. Add onion and garlic and sauté for 1-2 minutes. Add the cinnamon stick and sauté until fragrant.
3. Add the carrot, potato, red pepper, raisins, eggplant, and zucchini. Season with salt and cook for 3 to 4 minutes, stirring frequently.
4. Heat some olive oil in another pan and sauté mushrooms for a couple of minutes. Add to the vegetables.
5. Add the cumin and coriander and stir well.
6. Stir in the garbanzo beans, tomato puree and sugar, put the lid on and cook for 5 minutes over low heat. Once the vegetables are crisp-tender, add the chopped parsley and let cook for another 3-4 minutes, covered.
7. Remove from the heat and let stand 15 minutes before serving.

Couscous Shepherd's Pie

This dish is perfect for any gathering. The combination of couscous, carrots and Ras el hanout promise an interesting experience.

Prep time: 10 minutes
Cook time: 1hr 25 minutes
Serves 8
Ingredients:
4 tablespoons olive oil, divided
1 small onion, thinly sliced (1 cup)
3–4 tablespoons ras el hanout
2 15-oz. cans crushed tomatoes
4 carrots, cut (1 cup)
1 turnip, cut (1 cup)
2 zucchini, cut (1 cup)
1 ½ cups cooked chickpeas, or 1 15-oz. can chickpeas, rinsed and drained, divided
1 ½ cups couscous
1 tsp. salt
Directions:

1. Add 2 tablespoons of oil to a saucepan and set over medium heat. Add the onion, and cook 5 minutes, until tender.
2. Add Ras el Hanout, and cook 1 minute, or until it becomes brown.
3. Add 3 cups water and tomatoes, season with salt and pepper and bring to a simmer over medium-low heat, 18-20 minutes.
4. Stir in the turnip and carrots, put the lid on and cook about 10 minutes.
5. Add 3/4 cup chickpeas and zucchini and cook for another 5 minutes.
6. Place the remaining 3/4 cup chickpeas in a blender and pulse

until puree. Combine with the vegetable mixture, season with salt and pepper.
7. Transfer the vegetable mixture to a 13 x 9-inch baking dish.
8. Preheat oven to 350°F (175 °C). Place the couscous and salt in large heat-proof bowl, pour in 3 cups of boiling water, and let stand 5-10 minutes, until all water is absorbed.
9. Fluff the couscous with fork, and add the remaining 2 tablespoons oil.
10. Spoon the couscous over vegetable mixture and spread evenly.
11. Bake in the oven, until golden on top, about 25- 30 minutes.

Sweet Moroccan Glazed Tofu

This is an absolutely delicious dish and is perfect for any time of the day! Sure, it will make you a tofu lover once you try it.

Prep time: 7 minutes
Cook time: 7 minutes
Serves 4

Ingredients:
12 oz (330 g). Extra-firmtofu drained and pressed
1 teaspoon black pepper
1 teaspoon paprika
1 teaspoon salt
1/2 teaspoon cumin
1/4 teaspoon allspice
1 cup vegetable broth
1 medium carrot, chopped
1/2 cup frozen peas
1 tsp. olive oil
3/4 cup couscous
2 tbsp. canola oil
1/4 cup agave syrup

Directions:

1. Thinly slice the tofu and put them onto a large plate.
2. Combine the allspice, paprika, cumin, salt and pepper in a small bowl and sprinkle over the tofu, so it is evenly coated.
3. Add the peas, carrots, olive oil and vegetable broth to a large pot and bring to a boil. Stir in the couscous, season with 1/2 tsp salt and remove the pot from the heat.
4. Let stand for about 5 minutes, until all liquid is absorbed.
5. Add the agave and canola oil to a skillet and set over medium-high heat. Once it bubbles, add the sliced tofu, spiced side

down and cook for 3-4 minutes.
6. Gently turn over to cook the other side, too, 3 minutes more.
7. Fluff the couscous with a fork. Transfer it to a serving bowl and top with the done tofu.
8. Enjoy.

Vegan Berber Pizza

This is a vegan version for Medfouna. It is a Berber flatbread, stuffed with olives, herbs, onions and lots of spices

Prep Time: 30 minutes
Cook Time: 25 minutes
Serves 4-6

.

Ingredients

4 cups flour (some wheat, if desired)
2 teaspoons salt
2 teaspoons sugar
2 tablespoons olive oil
1 tablespoon yeast
1 1/4 cups warm water
For the Filling
2 lbs. (about 900 g) onions, chopped
1 bell pepper (any color), chopped
2 tablespoons olive oil
1 to 1 1/2 cups pitted green olives, sliced
2 handfuls of fresh parsley, chopped
2 tablespoons fresh thyme
1 teaspoon paprika
1 teaspoon cumin
1 teaspoon ground coriander
1/2 teaspoon ground red pepper (or to taste)
Salt and pepper (to taste)
1/2 teaspoon sugar (optional)
Olive oil,
Salt
Herbs for garnish (optional)

Directions:

1. In a large bowl, combine the flour, salt and sugar. In the center of the flour mixture, make a large hole and add the yeast.
2. Pour also the water and olive oil into the hole, and mix with a whisk, until the yeast is dissolved.
3. Then the dough is formed, transfer it to working surface, dusted with flour and knead with hands to make smooth and elastic dough.
4. Shape 2 balls, coat their surface with olive oil and let rise for about 40-45 minutes, covered with kitchen towel.
5. Start making the filling. Add the olive to a large frying pan and heat over medium heat.
6. Add the bell pepper and onions and cook until the onions have just softened, about 7 minutes. Remove the pan onions from the heat. Add the olives, herbs and spices, mix well and set aside.
7. Preheat an oven to 435°F (225°C).
8. Using a rolling pin, roll out one ball of the risen dough into a large round. Coat a baking sheet with oil and place the dough onto it.
9. Spoon the onion filling in the center, and spread evenly leaving at least 1/2" of dough exposed all around. Brush the exposed edge of dough with a little water.
10. Roll out the second ball of dough into round and put over the filling.
11. Lightly press the edges of the dough until sealed. Coat the dough with olive oil, season with salt and herbs.
12. Bake in the oven until golden brown, about 20 minutes. Transfer to a rack and let cool slightly. Serve warm.

Desserts

Oranges with Caramel and Cardamom Syrup

Cardamom pods and orange-flower water make this dessert so flavorful, moist and light that one can hardly stand the wish of taking the second portion.

Prep time: 35 minutes
Cook time: 12 minutes
6 servings
Ingredients:
1/2 cup water
2 cardamom pods, crushed
6 tablespoons sugar
5 medium navel oranges
2 tablespoons honey

1/8 teaspoon orange-flower water
Mint sprigs (optional)

Directions:

1. Add the cardamom and 1/2 cup water to a small heavy pot and set over medium-high heat.
2. Once the mixture boils, remove the pot from the heat and let stand, covered, for about 25 minutes.
3. Strain the mixture through a fine sieve and discard solids.
4. Add 1 tablespoon cardamom water and sugar to a skillet and place over medium heat. Cook for 7-8 minutes until sugar is melted and golden, without stirring.
5. Increase the heat to medium-high, and cook for another minute until the mixture becomes dark.
6. Remove from heat; gently pour the remaining cardamom water into the skillet and set back over medium-high heat, stirring constantly.
7. Using a paring knife, peel the oranges and cut crosswise into 6 slices each.
8. Place the slices on a rimmed dish and spoon hot syrup over oranges.
9. Refrigerate overnight, covered.
10. In a small bowl combine the honey and orange-flower water.
11. Garnish the oranges with mint sprigs and serve with honey mixture.

Moroccan Peaches

This is really a very amazing delicacy, which might become one of your favorites for treating your Moroccan guests.

Prep Time: 10 minutes
Cook Time: 2 hrs
Servings: 8
Ingredients:
8 largepeaches, ripe
3 tablespoonssuperfine sugar
8 teaspoonsrose water
Fresh mint leaves, to decorate
Directions:

1. Using a paring knife, peel the peaches and remove the pit. Cut each peach into 4-6 wedges and transfer to a serving bowl.
2. Spoon the rosewater over the peaches, sprinkle with sugar and place the bowl into the refrigerator for 2 hours, covered.
3. Garnish the peaches with mint leaves and enjoy.

1.

Moroccan Apple Dessert

Only the taste of these apples, flavored with cinnamon, lemons and orange blossom water worth the time spent in the kitchen.

Prep Time: 20 minutes
Cook Time: 15 minutes
Servings: 6-8

Ingredients:
8 tart apples, peeled cored and sliced in 8-10 wedges
3 lemons
2 cups sugar
2 cups water
2 tablespoons cinnamon
2 -4 tablespoons orange blossom water

Directions:

1. Peel the lemon and slice the rind into thin strips.
2. Juice the peeled lemons and reserve 1/2 cup of juice for later use.
3. Remove the peel and core from the apples and cut each into 8 to10 wedges.
4. Add the water, sugar, and cinnamon to a large pot and set over moderate heat.
5. Once it boils, stir in the lemon rind, apples, orange blossom water and lemon juice.
6. Let the mixture cook until the lemon rind and apples are soft and all liquid has evaporated.
7. Remove the pot from heat and let stand for 30 minutes before serving.

Moroccan Charoset Balls

Making these charosetballsis a real party for whole family. Make sure the kids are not around, as they will eat out all the balls before your guests arrive. Chill them for a while and enjoy.

Prep Time: 1 hr 15 minutes
Cook Time: 0 minutes
Serves 3-4
Ingredients:
2 cupspitted dates
1/2cupgolden raisin
1/2cupdark raisin
1/2cupwalnuts
1 -2 tablespoonsweet red wine

Directions:

1. Place the raisins, dates, walnuts in a food processor and pulse until finely chopped.
2. Add the wine and blend to get a sticky paste.
3. Place rounded teaspoonfuls of paste onto a baking sheet lined with wax paper.
4. Moisten your hands and roll each portion into a 1-inch ball.
5. Chill for 1-2 hours before serving.

Moroccan Cinnamon Cookies - Montecaos

Enjoy these extremely delicious and gorgeous looking cinnamon cookies with a cup of Moroccan mint tea.

Prep time: 10 minutes
Cook time: 20 minutes
Serves: 60
Ingredients:
1 cup vegetable oil
1⅓ cup confectioner's sugar
2 cups almond flour
2 cups whole wheat pastry flour
¼ tsp. salt
½ tsp. baking powder
1 tbsp. cinnamon
Directions:

1. Preheat oven at 325 °F (160 °C).
2. Place the sugar and oil in a large bowl and whisk well until the sugar is dissolved. Whisk in the almond flour.
3. In another bowl, place together the flour, baking powder, cinnamon and salt, slightly mix and add to the sugar mixture. Using a wooden spoon, mix well. Then knead the mixture with hands to form elastic dough.
4. Shape 60 small balls and arrange on the baking sheet, lined with parchment.
5. Bake in the preheated oven for 20 minutes until golden. Remove from the oven and let cool. Sprinkle the cookies with cinnamon and serve.

Sfenj-Moroccan Doughnuts

These simple doughnuts are a favorite treat in Morocco. I usually divide the dough, fry half of the doughnuts, and refrigerate the rest always to make a fresh treat. Coated with granulated sugar they make a great weekend breakfast.

Prep time: 1 hr 15 minutes
Cook time: 20 minutes
Makes 40 small doughnuts

Ingredients:
2.2lbs (I kg) all purpose flour
1 oz. (25 g) active dry yeast
3 1/3 cups lukewarm water
2/3 cup sugar
1 teaspoon salt
Canola oil for deep frying
Bit of canola oil for forming the dough
Sugar for coating

Directions:

1. Combine the yeast, sugar and water in small bowl and mix well.
2. In a large bowl, mix together the flour and salt.
3. Pour in the yeast mixture and knead well with your hands to get sticky dough. Cover the bowl with plastic wrap and place in a warm corner to rise for 1-2 hours until the dough doubles or triples its volume.
4. Add the canola oil to a large griddle and set over moderate heat. Once sizzling. Coat your hands with oil and take plum size dough .Using your index finger make a hole in the ball of dough and stretch the hole wide to make a ring.
5. Transfer the dough to the hot griddle and fry for about 2-3

minutes per side until golden. Transfer to paper towels to drain.
6. Repeat the process with the remaining dough.
7. Coat the doughnuts with granulated sugar and serve immediately.

Moroccan Sesame Seed cookies

These sesame seed cookies are easy to make and taste delicious. Serve them with fresh made fruit salad and satisfy your sweet tooth in the healthiest way.

Prep time: 30 minutes
Cook time: 25 minutes
Makes 36 cookies
Ingredients:
3 cups sesame seeds
2 ½ cups flour
1 cup vegetable oil
1 cup water
1 cup granulated sugar
1 teaspoon vanilla
1 ½ teaspoons baking powder
Directions:

1. Combine the flour, sugar, sesame seeds and vanilla in a large bowl.
2. Add the oil and mix well. Then gradually add the water and continue mixing until smooth and a bit sticky.
3. Preheat the oven to 325 °F (165 °C). Line a baking sheet with parchment.
4. Split the dough into 3 balls and chill for 25 minutes.
5. Roll out the dough into a thin rectangle on a piece of parchment paper. Cut the dough into cookie shapes with a cookie cutter. Repeat this with the remaining balls.
6. Arrange the cookies on the baking sheet and bake in the oven for 22-25 minutes until lightly golden.

Moroccan Date Bonbons

These amazing bonbons are flavored with tons of spices and healthy nuts. Coat them with pistachio powder to make the chef-d'oeuvre complete.

Prep time: 25 minutes
Cook time: 4 minutes
Makes 30 bonbons
Ingredients:
1/2 cup plus 2 tablespoons sliced almonds
1/2 cup shelled pistachios
3/4 cup chopped walnuts
1 pound moist pitted dates, chopped
4 pitted kalamata or dry-cured Moroccan olives, chopped
1/2 tablespoon finely grated fresh ginger
1/2 tablespoon honey
1/2 teaspoon orange zest, finely grated
1/4 teaspoon cinnamon
1/8 teaspoon ground cardamom
1/8 teaspoon orange flower water
1/8 teaspoon salt
Directions:

1. Preheat the oven to 350°F (170 °C). Place the sliced almonds on a baking tray and toast for about 3-4 minutes, until fragrant and golden. Let cool completely.
2. Place the pistachios in a food processor and pulse until coarsely ground.
3. Remove the ground pistachio from the food processor and grind the toasted almonds in the processor.
4. Add the dates, walnuts, olives, ginger, orange zest, honey, cardamom, cinnamon, orange flower water and salt and pulse

until paste.
5. Moisten your hands and shape about 30 balls. Gently roll the bonbons in the pistachio powder until evenly coated.
6. Enjoy.

Honey Almond Stuffed Dates

One-two steps and these wonderful honey almond dates are ready to be served. They will create a pleasant atmosphere along with a cup of tea or coffee.

Prep time: 5 minutes
Cook time: 10 minutes
Makes 20 filled dates
Ingredients:
20 dates
20 almonds
2 tsp honey
Directions:

1. Place the almonds in a small skillet and toast over medium-low heat until fragrant and light golden, 3-4 minutes.
2. Remove from the heat and stir in the honey. Return the skillet back to the heat and let cook until almonds are caramelized, 5 minutes.
3. Place still hot almonds onto a piece of baking parchment and gently with a fork. Let cool.
4. Halve the dates in lengthways and remove the pit. Place a sticky almond in the hole of each date and gently press the date on both sides with fingers.

Conclusion

I believe that with this cookbook we could transfer you the real spirit of Moroccan cuisine, to feel the real color and flavor of Morocco.

With a basic knowledge of cooking tweaks and techniques, you can prepare healthy vegan soups, salads, stews or desserts and enjoy at the table with your family.

If you went through the recipes and had a chance to taste them you have noticed that Moroccan cuisine is rich in fresh vegetables, fruits, grains, olive oil, beans, herbs and spices and it offers wide variety of options for vegan people, or for those who intend to increase vegetables in their diet.

Thank you once again for choosing this cookbook and good luck.

Don't miss out!

Visit the website below and you can sign up to receive emails whenever Bryan Rylee publishes a new book. There's no charge and no obligation.

https://books2read.com/r/B-A-FTAH-UISV

BOOKS 2 READ

Connecting independent readers to independent writers.

www.ingramcontent.com/pod-product-compliance
Ingram Content Group UK Ltd.
Pitfield, Milton Keynes, MK11 3LW, UK
UKHW031925060125
453151UK00001B/45